Simple Machines

Steck
Vaughn™

HOUGHTON MIFFLIN HARCOURT
Supplemental Publishers

www.SteckVaughn.com
800-531-5015

Simple Machines

contents

Simple Machines
Fact Matters

ISBN-13: 978-1-4190-5457-0
ISBN-10: 1-4190-5457-0

First published by Blake Education Pty Ltd as *Go Facts*
Copyright © 2006 Blake Publishing
This edition copyright under license from Blake Education Pty Ltd
© 2010 Steck-Vaughn, an imprint of HMH Supplemental Publishers Inc.

What Is a Simple Machine?

A machine is a tool that makes work easier. A simple machine is a simple tool.

Work occurs when a **force** makes something move. Lifting a heavy box out of a truck requires work. It needs a lifting force. It's easier to slide the box down a ramp. A ramp is a simple machine.

A simple machine does not reduce the amount of work needed. It spreads the force over a longer distance. This makes the work easier. Simple machines can also change the direction or speed of a force.

A simple machine has only a few moving parts. Some simple machines have no moving parts.

There are two main types of simple machines. They are **inclined** planes and **levers**. Ramps, wedges, and screws are types of inclined planes. Pulleys and wheels and axles are types of levers.

We use simple machines every day. Opening a door uses simple machines. So does turning on a faucet and walking up stairs.

Many activities **rely** on simple machines.

screw

4

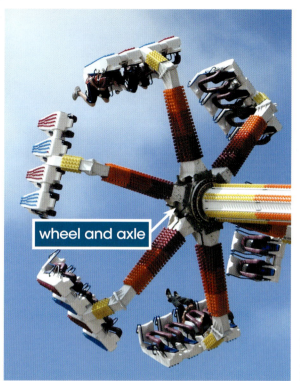

wheel and axle

wedge

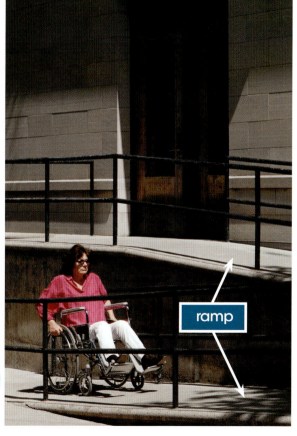

ramp

pulley

Inclined Planes

An inclined plane is a flat surface with one end higher than the other.

An inclined plane is one of the simplest kinds of machines. Inclined planes reduce the force needed to raise something.

Steep inclined planes need great force to push an object up. The flatter the **slope**, the less force needed. But you have to push objects farther to get to the same height.

Stairs and sloped paths are inclined planes. It is easier to walk up a long, gentle hill than to climb up a short, steep hill.

Escalators, boat ramps, ski jumps, and ladders are all inclined planes.

Roads that wind over a mountain are inclined planes. Cars have to travel farther to get to the top.

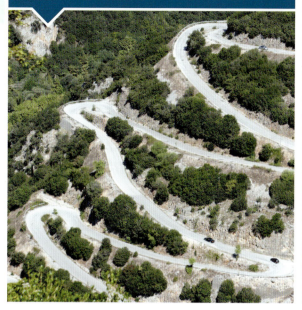

It is easier to walk up stairs than to climb straight up a building.

The ancient Egyptians used ramps to build the Great Pyramid of Giza.

Wedges

A wedge changes the direction of a force.

When a force pushes on a wedge, the wedge makes the force go in two directions.

A single wedge looks like an inclined plane. It has one sloping surface. A doorstop is a single wedge. It pushes the door and floor apart.

A double wedge has two inclined planes back to back. It has two sloping surfaces. The head of an ax is a double wedge.

A kitchen knife is a double wedge. Its cutting power depends on how sharp and thick it is.

A nail is also a wedge. The sharp tip of the nail pushes wood apart. This makes it easier to hammer the nail into something.

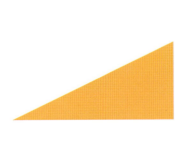

single wedge

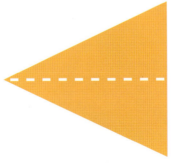

double wedge

A cutting edge is a wedge.

Your sharp front teeth are also wedges.

Did You Know?

The sharper a wedge is, the better it cuts. In 1999, a 13-inch log was chopped in just 12.5 seconds.

The bow of a boat is a wedge. It divides water.

Screws

Screws hold things together. They can also lower and raise objects.

A screw is an inclined plane wrapped around a **cylinder**. This inclined plane forms a ridge along the cylinder. This ridge is called the **thread** of the screw.

A screw is turned by a screwdriver. The screw turns a greater distance than it moves forward. The turning motion becomes a forward motion.

The Greek mathematician Archimedes invented a screw machine more than 2,200 years ago. It was used to lift water. The machine contained a long screw inside of a pipe. One end sat in the water. As the machine was turned, water was scooped into the turning thread. The water was carried to the top of the screw. It then flowed out of a hole at the top. The screw machine was used to lift water into fields and out of ships.

The screw makes a vise close tightly.

A spiral staircase is a type of screw. It is easier to climb one than to walk up a straight staircase.

This screw crushes grapes.

The closer together the threads, the easier it is to turn a screw.

Did You Know?

One type of propeller is called a screw propeller. It looks like a long screw underneath a boat. It **provides** a push force through the water.

Levers

*Levers lift or move **loads**. They are one of the most common simple machines. Almost every object with a handle acts as a lever.*

A lever is a stiff bar or board that rests on a point. The bar or board turns on the point. This point is called a **fulcrum**.

If you push or pull on one end of the lever, you apply a force. The other end of the lever goes in the opposite direction. The object that a lever moves is called the load.

If the fulcrum is close to the load, less force is needed to lift the load. The load moves a shorter distance than the force.

If the fulcrum is close to the force, greater force is needed to lift the load. The load moves a greater distance than the force.

A hammer is a first-class lever when it is used to pull out a nail.

There are three classes of levers. The class depends on the positions of the fulcrum, load, and force.

first class

The fulcrum is located between the force and the load.

second class

The load is located between the fulcrum and the force.

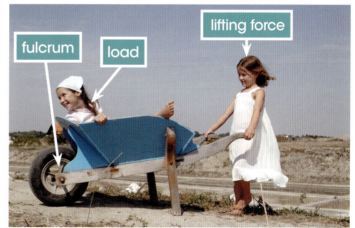

third class

The force is located between the fulcrum and the load.

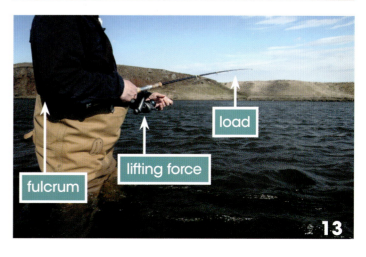

Working with Levers

What's the easiest way to break a toothpick or crack a nut?

What you need:

- a toothpick
- a nutcracker
- a hard nut

1 Place a toothpick across the back of your middle finger, just below your fingernail. The ends should rest underneath your first and third fingers. Try to break the toothpick by pressing down with your first and third fingers.

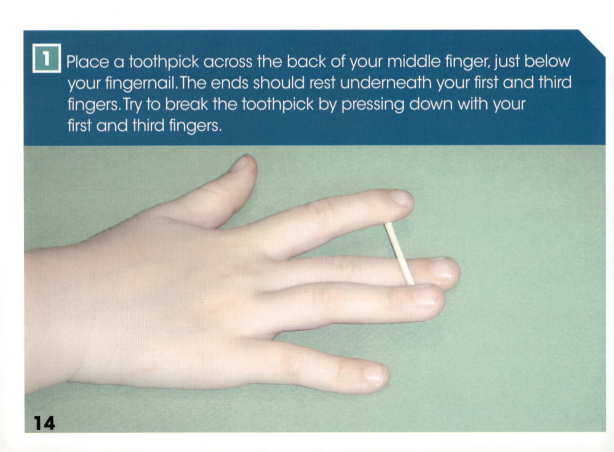

2 Move the toothpick closer to your knuckle. Try to break the toothpick with your fingers again. The fulcrum is your knuckle.

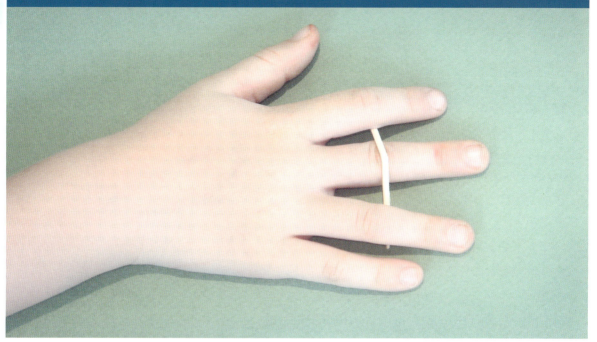

3 Now try to crack a nut with the nutcracker. First try cracking it with the nut at the far end of the nutcracker, closest to your hands. Then move the nut closer to the joint of the nutcracker. This is the fulcrum.

The farther away the toothpick and nut are from the fulcrum, the more force is needed to break them.

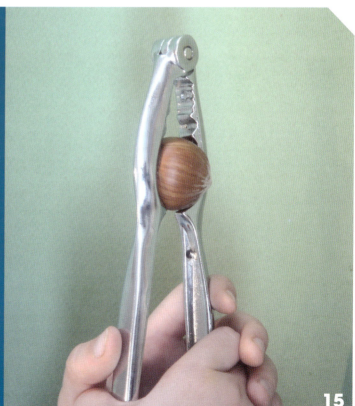

Pulleys

A pulley uses a wheel and a rope to move a load. A pulley increases a force or changes its direction.

A simple pulley has one wheel. A rope runs through a groove on the wheel. One end of the rope is tied to a load. A force pulls on the other end. Simple pulleys are generally used on blinds and sailboats.

A rope can run through more than one pulley. With two pulleys, only half the force is needed to lift a load. The rope has to be pulled twice as far. With three pulleys, only one-third of the force is needed. The rope has to be pulled three times as far.

A **compound** pulley has more than one wheel. It is also called a block and tackle. The more pulleys used, the easier it is to move the load.

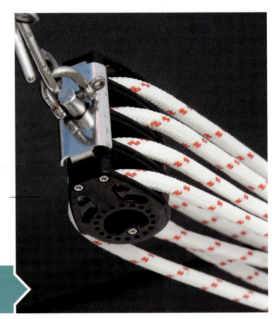

compound pulley

A pulley can change the direction of a force.

pull down the rope

flags go up

Ropes and pulleys can help one person lift another person.

A crane using pulleys can lift almost anything.

17

Wheels and Axles

A wheel can lift and move loads.

A rod that runs through the middle of the wheel is called an **axle**. The axle is joined to the wheel. When the wheel or axle turns, the other part also turns. The steering wheel in a car is a wheel and axle.

The circle turned by the wheel is much larger than the circle turned by the axle. The longer distance turned by the wheel causes the axle to turn more powerfully.

A wheel and axle is often used with **gears**. A gear is a wheel with **cogs** around its edge. Several gears can be connected. Their cogs lock into each other. The gears can be different sizes. When one gear turns, it makes the other gears turn.

Wheelchairs have wheels and axles.

wheel

axle

Did You Know?

A Ferris wheel is a large wheel and axle. One Ferris wheel in China is 525 feet high. Another in Singapore is 541 feet high.

If one gear turned, which way would the others turn?

A bicycle has gears of many different sizes.

Compound Machines

*A **compound machine** is made from two or more simple machines that work together as one.*

Many of the machines we use every day are compound machines.

A shovel is a compound machine. The handle is a lever. The blade is a wedge. A can opener is made up of levers, a wedge, and a wheel and axle. Even **complex** machines, such as cars or airplanes, are based on the six simple machines.

All of the objects on these pages are compound machines.

lever

wheel and axle

wedge

lever

wheel and axle

lever

screw

lever

lever

lever

pulley

wheel and axle

21

Simple Machines at Work

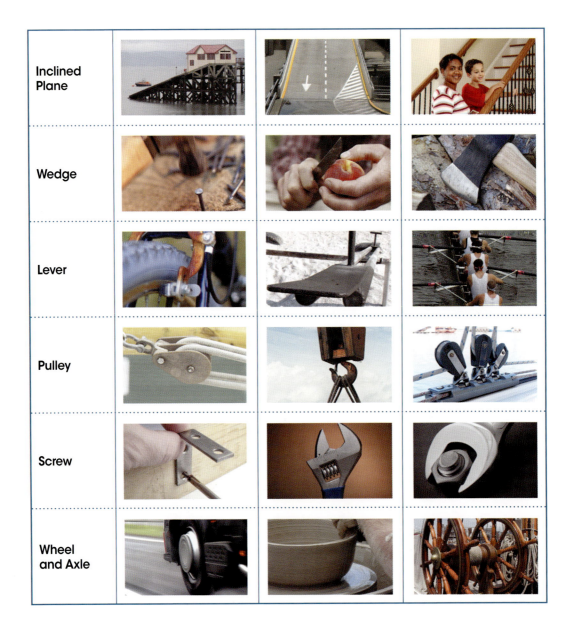

Inclined Plane			
Wedge			
Lever			
Pulley			
Screw			
Wheel and Axle			

Glossary

axle (AK suhl) a rod through the middle of a wheel

cog (kog) a tooth located on the edge of a gear

complex (kom PLEHKS) made up of many different parts

compound (KOM pownd) made up of two or more parts

compound machine (KOM pownd muh SHEEN) two or more simple machines that work as one machine

cylinder (SIHL uhn duhr) a tube with long, straight sides and two circular ends

force (fohrs) a push or pull that changes the speed, direction, or shape of something

fulcrum (FUHL kruhm) the point on which a lever turns

gear (gihr) a wheel with teeth around the edge; connects to other gears

inclined (ihn KLYND) when one end of something is higher than the other

lever (LEHV uhr) a bar which rests on a fulcrum and is used to transmit force

load (lohd) the weight to be supported or moved

provides (pruh VYDZ) gives or creates

rely (rih LY) to depend on something

slope (slohp) a flat surface with one end higher than the other

thread (threhd) a ridge that goes around the outside of a screw

Index